Dear Rachel

Happ

& Luca
x x x

Leunig

When I talk to You

A CARTOONIST TALKS TO GOD

HarperCollins*Publishers*

Love is like bread.
It has to be made fresh every day.
Old saying

Acknowledgments

The title of this book comes from Mary Phil Korsak, who translated my first prayer collection, *A Common Prayer*, into French (*Prieres d'en rire*, published in Paris by Les Editions de l'Atelier, 2003). 'Quand je te parle' was her carefully chosen working title for the translation, and the English approximation, 'When I talk to you', seemed to fit beautifully as a title for this combined work. Profound thanks to Mary Phil in Brussels for these words.

I also want to acknowledge the beloved presence of Anne Clancy and Helga Salwe in the making of these prayers. It was through them that I found the words in this book.

Preface

The prayers contained in this book were created for publication in Melbourne's *Sunday Age* newspaper. Their publication was something of a small experiment both for myself and the paper.

I was originally asked to draw a weekly cartoon but found it difficult to be enthused. I felt there were already enough jokes and amusements at hand and the boom in humour and satire at the time struck me as somewhat oppressive. It seemed to me that newspapers might carry some small spiritual message of consolation as a tiny reparation for the enormous anxiety and distress I believe they create, an anxiety and distress which I felt was not and could not be sufficiently addressed or relieved by humorists. I was losing my faith in professional humour.

Prayer as a creative lacuna, as an ancient free form and as a marvellous, stabilising idea, intrigued me greatly. The spirit of the times, so constricted by fashion anxiety, so repressed by information, ego and scientific authority, seemed the ideal climate for the cultivation of public prayers.

The presence of any sincere prayer (and as Mark Twain observed, 'You can't pray a lie') in the realm of contemporary journalism was likely to create a small, embarrassing and healthy juxtaposition, and knowing that such juxtapositions must *always* be attempted, I set out awkwardly to write prayers for the newspaper. All I hoped was that my efforts might help revitalise the *idea* of prayer for those who had abandoned it or never considered it at all. I also wanted to gently foster the notion that the mass media might take on a measure of spiritual responsibility by publishing a small weekly tribute to innocence. I opened my heart to derision. I learned much as I proceeded.

The nature and the words of the particular prayers in this book are perhaps not as important as the idea of prayer itself. After all, these are public prayers, which makes them seem a bit impersonal and contrived. Some of them are expressions of hope, some are declarations, others are thanksgivings. Their creation has involved feelings of considerable vulnerability, because I understand that such things are readily and gladly misunderstood. They are my fumbling experiments and they mostly derive from a situation of deep personal struggle which was difficult, wonderful and radical.

The book, however, is offered as something of a prayer itself. I hope it somehow contributes to the illumination of this small, ancient, wonderful, free-form, do-it-yourself ritual of connection, love and transformation: the common prayer.

Introduction

I have drawn a simple picture of a person kneeling before a duck to symbolise and demonstrate my ideas and feelings about the nature of prayer. I ask the reader to bear with the absurdity of the image and to remember that the search for the sublime may sometimes have a ridiculous beginning. Here then is the story behind the picture.

A man kneels before a duck in a sincere attempt to talk with it. This is a clear depiction of irrational behaviour and an important aspect of prayer. Let us put this aside for the moment and move on to the particulars.

The act of kneeling in the picture symbolises humility. The upright stance has been abandoned because of the human attitudes and qualities it represents: power, stature, control, rationality, worldliness, pride and ego. The kneeling man knows, as everybody does, that a proud and upright man does not and cannot talk with a duck. So the upright stance is rejected. The man kneels. He humbles himself. He comes closer to the duck. He becomes more like the duck. He does these things because it improves his chances of communicating with it.

The duck in the picture symbolises one thing and many things: nature, instinct, feeling, beauty, innocence, the primal, the non-rational and the mysterious unsayable; qualities we can easily attribute to a duck and qualities which, coincidentally and remarkably, we can easily attribute to the inner life of the kneeling man, to his spirit or his soul. The duck then, in this picture, can be seen as a symbol of the human spirit, and in wanting connection with his spirit it is a symbolic picture of a man searching for his soul.

The person cannot actually see this 'soul' as he sees the duck but he can feel its enormous impact on his life. Its outward manifestations can be disturbing and dramatic and its inner presence is often wild and rebellious or elusive and difficult to grasp: but the person knows that from this inner dimension, with all its turmoil, comes his love and his fear, his creative spark, his music, his art and his very will to live. He also feels that a strong relationship with this inner world seems to lead to a good relationship with the world around him and a better life. Conversely, he feels that alienation from these qualities, or loss of spirit, seems to cause great misery and loneliness.

He believes in this spiritual dimension, this inner life, and he knows that it can be strengthened by acknowledgment and by giving it a name.

He may call it the human spirit, he may call it the soul or he may call it god. The particular name is not so very important.

The point is that he acknowledges this spiritual dimension. He would be a fool to ignore it, so powerful is its effect on his life, so joyous, so mysterious, so frightening.

Not only does he recognise and name it but he is intensely curious about it. He wants to explore it and familiarise himself with its ways and its depth. He wants a robust relationship with it, he wants to trust it, he wants its advice and the vitality it provides. He also wants to feed it, this inner world, to care for it and make it strong. It's important to him.

And the more he does these things, this coming to terms with his soul, the more his life takes on a sense of meaning. The search for the spirit leads to love and a better world, for him and for those around him. This personal act is also a social and political act because it affects so many people who may be connected to the searcher.

But how do we search for our soul, our god, our inner voice? How do we find this treasure hidden in our life? How do we connect to this transforming and healing power? It seems as difficult as talking to a bird. How indeed?

There are many ways, all of them involving great struggle, and each person must find his or her own way. The search and the relationship is a lifetime's work and there is much help available, but an important, perhaps essential part of this process seems to involve an ongoing, humble acknowledgment of the soul's existence and integrity. Not just an intellectual recognition but also a ritualistic, perhaps poetic, gesture of acknowledgment: a respectful tribute.

Why it should need to be like this is mysterious, but a ceremonial affirmation, no matter how small, seems to carry an indelible and resonant quality into the heart which the intellect is incapable of carrying.

Shaking the hand of a friend is such a ritual. It reaffirms something deep and unsayable in the relationship. A non-rational ritual acknowledges and reaffirms a non-rational, but important, part of the relationship. It is a small but vital thing.

This ritual of recognition and connection is repeatable and each time it occurs something important is revitalised and strengthened. The garden is watered.

And so it is with the little ritual which recognises the inner life and attempts to connect to it. This do-it-yourself ceremony where the mind is on its knees; the small ceremony of words which calls on the soul to come forth. This ritual known simply as prayer.

The garden is watered.

A person kneels before a duck and speaks to it with sincerity. The person is praying.

Love is born
With a dark and troubled face
When hope is dead
And in the most unlikely place
Love is born:
Love is always born.

God help us to change. To change ourselves and to change our world. To know the need for it. To deal with the pain of it. To feel the joy of it. To undertake the journey without understanding the destination. The art of gentle revolution.

Amen.

God let us be serious.
Face to face.
Heart to heart.
Let us be fully present.
Strongly present.
Deeply serious.
The closest we may come
to innocence.

Amen.

God give us rain when we expect sun.
Give us music when we expect trouble.
Give us tears when we expect breakfast.
Give us dreams when we expect a storm.
Give us a stray dog when we expect congratulations.
God play with us, turn us sideways and around.

Amen.

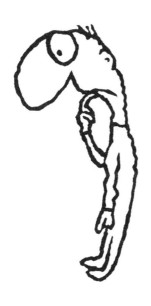

Dear God,

We celebrate spring's returning and the rejuvenation
of the natural world. Let us be moved by this vast
and gentle insistence that goodness shall return,
that warmth and life shall succeed, and help us to
understand our place within this miracle. Let us see
that as a bird now builds its nest, bravely, with bits and
pieces, so we must build human faith. It is our simple
duty; it is the highest art; it is our natural and vital role
within the miracle of spring: the creation of faith.

Amen.

God bless our contradictions, those parts of us
which seem out of character. Let us be boldly
and gladly out of character. Let us be creatures of
paradox and variety: creatures of contrast; of light
and shade: creatures of faith. God be our constant.
Let us step out of character into the unknown, to
struggle and love and do what we will.

Amen.

We give thanks for the life and work of Wolfgang Amadeus Mozart. Let us celebrate and praise all those musicians and composers who give their hands and hearts and voices to the expression of life's mystery and joy.

Who nourish our heart in its yearning.
Who dignify our soul in its struggling.
Who harmonise our grief and gladness.
Who make melody from the fragments of chaos.
Who align our spirit with creation.
Who reveal to us the grace of God.
Who calm us and delight us and set us free to love
        and forgive.
Let us give thanks and rejoice.

Amen.

Dear God,

We give thanks for birds. All types of birds. Small birds and large birds. Domestic fowls, migratory birds and birds of prey, hooting birds, whistling birds, shrikes, coloured parrots and dark darting wrens. Birds too numerous to mention. We praise them all.

We mourn the loss of certain species and pray for the deliverance of endangered ones. We pray, too, for farm birds, that they may be released from cruelty and suffering.

We give thanks for eggs and feathers, for brave, cheerful songs in the morning and the wonderful, haunting, night prayers of owls and all nocturnal fowls.

We praise the character of birds, their constancy,

their desire for freedom, their flair for music and talent for flying. May we always marvel at their ability to fly. Especially we praise their disregard for the human hierarchy and the ease with which they leave their droppings on the heads of commoners or kings regardless. Grant them fair weather, fresh food and abundant materials for building their nests in spring. Provide them too with perches and roosts with pleasant aspects. Dear God, guide our thoughts to the joy and beauty of birds. Feathered angels. May they always be above us.

Amen.

It is time to plant tomatoes. Dear God, we praise this fruit and give thanks for its life and evolution. We salute the tomato: cheery, fragrant morsel, beloved provider, survivor and thriver and giver of life. Giving and giving and giving. Plump with summer's joy. The scent of its stem is summer's joy, is promise and rapture. Its branches breathe perfume of promise and rapture. Giving and giving and giving.

Dear God, give strength to the wings and knees of pollinating bees, give protection from hailstorms, gales and frosts, give warm days and quenching rains. Refresh and adorn our gardens and our tables. Refresh us with tomatoes.

Rejoice and rejoice! Celebrate the scarlet soul of winter sauces. Behold the delicious flavour! Behold the oiled vermilion moons that ride and dive in olive-bobbing seas of vinegared lettuce. Let us rejoice! Let this rejoicing be our thanks for tomatoes.

Amen.

God help us with ideas, those thoughts which inform the way we live and the things we do. Let us not seize upon ideas, neither shall we hunt them down nor steal them away. Rather let us wait faithfully for them to approach, slowly and gently like creatures from the wild. And let them enter willingly into our hearts and come and go freely within the sanctuary of our contemplation, informing our souls as they arrive and being enlivened by the inspiration of our hearts as they leave. These shall be our truest thoughts. Our willing and effective ideas. Let us treasure their humble originality. Let us follow them gently back into the world with faith that they shall lead us to lives of harmony and integrity.

Amen.

God help us to find our confession;
The truth within us which is hidden from our mind;
The beauty or the ugliness we see elsewhere
But never in ourselves;
The stowaway which has been smuggled
Into the dark side of the heart,
Which puts the heart off balance and causes it pain,
Which wearies and confuses us,
Which tips us in false directions and inclines us
        to destruction,
The load which is not carried squarely
Because it is carried in ignorance.

God help us to find our confession.

Help us across the boundary of our understanding.

Lead us into the darkness that we may find what
    lies concealed;

That we may confess it towards the light;

That we may carry our truth in the centre of our heart;

That we may carry our cross wisely

And bring harmony into our life and our world.

Amen.

Dear God,

Give comfort and peace to those who are separated
from loved ones. May the ache in their hearts be
the strengthening of their hearts. May their longing
bring resolve to their lives, conviction and purity
to their love. Teach them to embrace their sadness
lest it turn to despair. Transform their yearning
into wisdom. Let their hearts grow fonder.

Amen.

God bless the lost, the confused,
the unsure, the bewildered, the puzzled,
the mystified, the baffled, and the perplexed.

Amen.

There are only two feelings.
    Love and fear.
There are only two languages.
    Love and fear.
There are only two activities.
    Love and fear.
There are only two motives,
two procedures, two frameworks,
two results.
    Love and fear.
Love and fear.

Dear God,

We give thanks for the darkness of the night
where lies the world of dreams. Guide us
closer to our dreams so that we may be
nourished by them. Give us strong dreams and
memory of them so that we may carry their
poetry and mystery into our daily lives.

　　Grant us deep and restful sleep that we may wake
refreshed with strength enough to renew a world
grown tired.

　　We give thanks for the inspiration of stars,
the dignity of the moon and the lullabies of crickets
and frogs.

　　Let us restore the night and reclaim it as a
sanctuary of peace, where silence shall be music to
our hearts and darkness shall throw light upon our
souls. Good night. Sweet dreams.

Amen.

God rest us.

Rest that part of us which is tired.

Awaken that part of us which is asleep.

God awaken us and awake within us.

Amen.

We give thanks for the mystery of hair.
Too little here and too much there.
Censored and shaved, controlled and suppressed:
Unwelcome guest in soups and sandwiches.
Difficult growth always needing attention.
Gentle and comforting;
Complex and wild;
Reminding us softly
That we might be animals.
Growing and growing
'Til the day that we die.
And the day after as well
So they say!
In all of its places
And in all of its ways
We give thanks for the blessing of hair.

Amen.

God be with those who explore in the cause
of understanding, whose search takes them far
from what is familiar and comfortable and leads
them into danger or terrifying loneliness. Let
us try to understand their sometimes strange
or difficult ways; their confronting or unusual
language; the uncommon life of their emotions,
for they have been affected and shaped and
changed by their struggle at the frontiers of a
wild darkness, just as we may be affected, shaped
and changed by the insights they bring back
to us. Bless them with strength and peace.

Amen.

In order to be truthful
We must do more than speak the truth.
We must also hear truth.
We must also receive truth.
We must also act upon truth.
We must also search for truth.
The difficult truth.
Within us and around us.

We must devote ourselves to truth.
Otherwise we are dishonest
And our lives are mistaken.
God grant us the strength and the courage
To be truthful.

Amen.

Dear God,

We pray for another way of being: another way of knowing.

Across the difficult terrain of our existence we have attempted to build a highway and in so doing have lost our footpath. God lead us to our footpath: lead us there where in simplicity we may move at the speed of natural creatures and feel the earth's love beneath our feet. Lead us there where step-by-step we may feel the movement of creation in our hearts. And lead us there where side-by-side we may feel the embrace of the common soul. Nothing can be loved at speed.

God lead us to the slow path; to the joyous insights of the pilgrim; another way of knowing: another way of being.

Amen.

God help us to live slowly:

To move simply:

To look softly:

To allow emptiness:

To let the heart create for us.

Amen.

Let us live in such a way
That when we die
Our love will survive
And continue to grow.

Amen.

God help us
To rise up from our struggle.
Like a tree rises up from the soil.
Our roots reaching down to our trouble,
Our rich, dark dirt of existence.
Finding nourishment deeply
And holding us firmly.
Always connected.
Growing upwards and into the sun.

Amen.

Let us pray for wisdom. Let us pause from thinking and empty our mind. Let us stop the noise. In the silence let us listen to our heart. The heart which is buried alive. Let us be still and wait and listen carefully. A sound from the deep, from below. A faint cry. A weak tapping. Distant muffled feelings from within. The cry for help.

We shall rescue the entombed heart. We shall bring it to the surface, to the light and the air. We shall nurse it and listen respectfully to its story. The heart's story of pain and suffocation, of darkness and yearning. We shall help our feelings to live in the sun. Together again we shall find relief and joy.

We welcome summer and the glorious blessing of light. We are rich with light; we are loved by the sun. Let us empty our hearts into the brilliance. Let us pour our darkness into the glorious, forgiving light. For this loving abundance let us give thanks and offer our joy.

Amen.

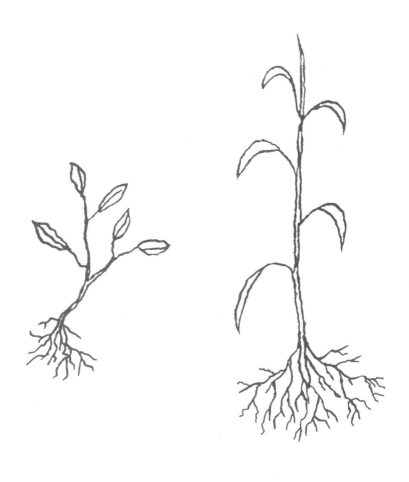

Dear God,

We pray for balance and exchange. Balance us like trees. As the roots of a tree shall equal its branches so must the inner life be equal to the outer life. And as the leaves shall nourish the roots so shall the roots give nourishment to the leaves. Without equality and exchange of nourishment there can be no growth and no love.

Amen.

Dear God,

We struggle, we grow weary, we grow tired. We are exhausted, we are distressed, we despair. We give up, we fall down, we let go. We cry. We are empty, we grow calm, we are ready. We wait quietly.

A small, shy truth arrives. Arrives from without and within. Arrives and is born. Simple, steady, clear. Like a mirror, like a bell, like a flame. Like rain in summer. A precious truth arrives and is born within us. Within our emptiness.

We accept it, we observe it, we absorb it. We surrender to our bare truth. We are nourished, we are changed. We are blessed. We rise up.

For this we give thanks.

Amen.

Dear God,

These circumstances will change.
This situation shall pass.

Amen.

Dear God,

We rejoice and give thanks for earthworms, bees,
ladybirds and broody hens; for humans tending their
gardens, talking to animals, cleaning their homes
and singing to themselves; for the rising of the
sap, the fragrance of growth, the invention of the
wheelbarrow and the existence of the teapot, we
give thanks. We celebrate and give thanks.

Amen.

We give thanks for singers.

All types of singers.

Popular, concert singers and tuneless
          singers in the bath.

Whistlers, hummers and those who sing
          while they work.

Singers of lullabies; singers of nonsense and
          small scraps of melody.

Singers on branches and rooftops.

Morning yodellers and evening warblers.

Singers in seedy nightclubs, singers in the street;

Singers in cathedrals, school halls, grandstands,
          back yards, paddocks, bedrooms, corridors,
          stairwells and places of echo and resonance.

We give praise to all those who give some small voice

To the everyday joy of the soul.

Amen.

God be with the mother. As she carried her child may she carry her soul. As her child was born, may she give birth and life and form to her own, higher truth. As she nourished and protected her child, may she nourish and protect her inner life and her independence. For her soul shall be her most painful birth, her most difficult child and the dearest sister to her other children.

Amen.

Autumn.

We give thanks for the harvest of the heart's work;
Seeds of faith planted with faith;
Love nurtured by love;
Courage strengthened by courage.
We give thanks for the fruits of the struggling soul,
The bitter and the sweet;
For that which has grown in adversity
And for that which has flourished in
     warmth and grace;
For the radiance of the spirit in autumn
And for that which must now fade and die.
We are blessed and give thanks.

Amen.

Dear God,

We give thanks for places of simplicity and peace.
Let us find such a place within ourselves. We give
thanks for places of refuge and beauty. Let us find
such a place within ourselves. We give thanks
for places of nature's truth and freedom, of joy,
inspiration and renewal, places where all creatures
may find acceptance and belonging. Let us search for
these places: in the world, in ourselves and in others.
Let us restore them. Let us strengthen and protect
them and let us create them.

   May we mend this outer world according to the
truth of our inner life and may our souls be shaped
and nourished by nature's eternal wisdom.

Amen.

God help us. With great skill and energy we have ignored the state of the human heart. With politics and economics we have denied the heart's needs. With eloquence, wit and reason we have belittled the heart's wisdom. With sophistication and style, with science and technology, we have drowned out the voice of the soul. The primitive voice, the innocent voice. The truth. We cannot hear our heart's truth and thus we have betrayed and belittled ourselves and pledged madness to our children. With skill and pride we have made for ourselves an unhappy society. God be with us.

Amen.

God be amongst us and within us. Earth is our
mother and nature's law is our father, our protector.
Thus, we pray.

Father do not forgive them for they know
precisely what they do. Those destroyers of earth's
beauty and goodness, those killers of nature, do not
forgive them.

Those betrayers of nature's love. Those exploiters
of nature's innocence. Those poisoners. Do not
forgive them.

Those greedy, pompous people. That greed and
pomposity within us all. The sum total of that petty
greed and pomposity within us all. We now know
precisely what these things are doing to this earth.
So Father, do not forgive us for we now understand
what it is that we do.

Amen.

Let us pray for the victims of war:

For the wounded and the dead.

For those who mourn and are afflicted.

For the earth and its innocent creatures —
Now mutilated and in disarray.

For the aggrieved and suffering souls —
Now bombed into submission and tormented silence.

For the scales of justice —
Now locked in false balance.

For the dove —
Now mocked by the metal wings of cruelty and greed.

For the yearnings and labours of peacemakers,
        healers and teachers —
Now degraded by the cunning and cowardice
        of warlike minds.

For the needy whose precious resources are now
        wasted and spent.

For the beautiful treasures, icons and holy places —
Now defiled by a crass science, now smashed by
        vulgar and heartless economies.

For those who seek to know what has befallen
        their world —
Now deceived and bewildered by the dictatorships
        of information.
We lament this poisoned and sorrowful state,
We resist this brutal invasion of the common soul.
We pray for peace.

Amen

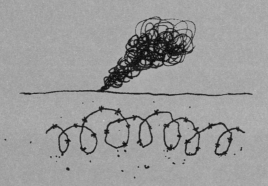

That which is Christ-like within us shall
be crucified. It shall suffer and be broken.
And that which is Christ-like within us
shall rise up. It shall love and create.

We give thanks for the invention of the handle. Without it there would be many things we couldn't hold on to. As for the things we can't hold on to anyway, let us gracefully accept their ungraspable nature and celebrate all things elusive, fleeting and intangible. They mystify us and make us receptive to truth and beauty. We celebrate and give thanks.

Amen.

We pray for the fragile ecology of the heart and the mind. The sense of meaning. So finely assembled and balanced and so easily overturned. The careful, ongoing construction of love. As painful and exhausting as the struggle for truth and as easily abandoned.

Hard fought and won are the shifting sands of this sacred ground, this ecology. Easy to desecrate and difficult to defend, this vulnerable joy, this exposed faith, this precious order. This sanity.

We shall be careful. With others and with ourselves.

Amen.

God bless the lone tunnellers; those rare individuals whose joy and passion it is to dig mysterious tunnels beneath the surface of the earth; who share the soulful purpose of moles and worms; who labour gleefully beneath our feet while we bask in the sun or gaze at the stars; whose pockets and cuffs are full of soil; who dig faithfully in darkness, turning left and turning right, not knowing why or where, but absorbed and fulfilled nevertheless. Under houses; under roads and statues; beneath and amongst the roots of trees; on elbows and knees; carefully, steadily pawing at their beloved earth; sniffing and savouring the rich odour of the dirt; dreaming and delighting in the blackness; onwards and onwards, not knowing day or night; unsung, unadorned, unassuming, unrestrained. Grimy fingernailed angels of the underworld: we praise them and give thanks for their constant, unseen presence and the vast labyrinth they have created beneath our existence. We praise them and give thanks.

Amen.

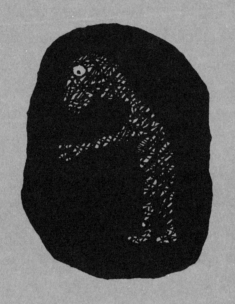

God help us

If our world should grow dark

And there is no way of seeing or knowing.

Grant us courage and trust

To touch and be touched

To find our way onwards

By feeling.

Amen.

Dear God,

Let us prepare for winter. The sun has turned away
from us and the nest of summer hangs broken in a
tree. Life slips through our fingers and, as darkness
gathers, our hands grow cold. It is time to go inside.
It is time for reflection and resonance. It is time for
contemplation. Let us go inside.

Amen.

We give thanks for the blessing of winter:
Season to cherish the heart.
To make warmth and quiet for the heart.
To make soups and broths for the heart.
To cook for the heart and read for the heart.
To curl up softly and nestle with the heart.
To sleep deeply and gently at one with the heart.
To dream with the heart.
To spend time with the heart.
A long, long time of peace with the heart.
We give thanks for the blessing of winter:
Season to cherish the heart.

Amen.

God bless those who suffer from the common cold.
Nature has entered into them;
Has led them aside and gently lain them low
To contemplate life from the wayside;
To consider human frailty;
To receive the deep and dreamy messages of fever.
We give thanks for the insights of
            this humble perspective.
We give thanks for blessings in disguise.

Amen.

We simplify our lives.

We live gladly with less.

We let go the illusion that we can possess.

We create instead.

We let go the illusion of mobility.

We travel in stillness. We travel at home.

By candlelight and in stillness,

In the presence of flowers,

We make our pilgrimage.

We simplify our lives.

God accept our prayers.
Send us tears in return.
Give freedom to this exchange.
Let us pray inwardly.
Let us weep outwardly.
This is the breathing of the soul.
This is the vitality of the spirit.
For this we give thanks.

Amen.

Dear God,

We loosen our grip.
We open our hand.
We are accepting.
In our empty hand
We feel the shape
Of simple eternity.
It nestles there.
We hold it gently.
We are accepting.

Amen.

We give thanks for domestic animals. Those
creatures who can trust us enough to come close.
Those creatures who can trust us enough to be true
to themselves.

They approach us from the wild. They approach
us from the inner world. They bring beauty and joy,
comfort and peace.

For this miracle and for the lesson of this miracle.
We give thanks.

Amen.

The path to your door
Is the path within:
Is made by animals,
Is lined by flowers,
Is lined by thorns,
Is stained with wine,
Is lit by the lamp of sorrowful dreams:
Is washed with joy,
Is swept by grief,
Is blessed by the lonely traffic of art:
Is known by heart,
Is known by prayer,
Is lost and found,
Is always strange,
The path to your door.

We give thanks for our friends.
Our dear friends.
We anger each other.
We fail each other.
We share this sad earth, this tender life,
          this precious time.
Such richness. Such wildness.
Together we are blown about.
Together we are dragged along.
All this delight.
All this suffering.
All this forgiving life.
We hold it together.

Amen.

God give us strength.
Strength to hold on and strength to let go.

Amen.

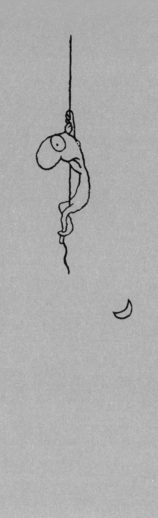

God bless this tiny little boat
And me who travels in it.
It stays afloat for years and years
And sinks within a minute.

And so the soul in which we sail,
Unknown by years of thinking,
Is deeply felt and understood
The minute that it's sinking.

We search and we search and yet find no meaning.
The search for a meaning leads to despair.
And when we are broken the heart finds its moment
To fly and to feel and to work as it will
Through the darkness and mystery and
        wild contradiction.
For this is its freedom, its need and its calling;
This is its magic, its strength and its knowing.
To heal and make meaning while we walk or
        lie dreaming;
To give birth to love within our surrender;
To mother our faith, our spirit and yearning;
While we stumble in darkness the heart makes
        our meaning
And offers it into our life and creation
That we may give meaning to life and creation
For we only give meaning we do not find meaning:
The thing we can't find is the thing we shall give.
To make love complete and to honour creation.

Dear God,

When we fall, let us fall inwards. Let us fall freely and completely: that we may find our depth and humility: the solid earth from which we may rise up and love again.

Amen.

When the heart
Is cut or cracked or broken
Do not clutch it
Let the wound lie open

Let the wind
From the good old sea blow in
To bathe the wound with salt
And let it sting.

Let a stray dog lick it
Let a bird lean in the hole and sing
A simple song like a tiny bell
And let it ring

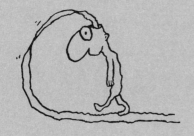

Let it go. Let it out.
Let it all unravel.
Let it free and it can be
A path on which to travel.

Christmas.

Dear God, it is timely that we give thanks for
the lives of all prophets, teachers, healers and
revolutionaries, living and dead, acclaimed or
obscure, who have rebelled, worked and suffered for
the cause of love and joy.

We also celebrate that part of us, that part within
ourselves, which has rebelled, worked and suffered
for the cause of love and joy.

We give thanks and celebrate.

Amen.

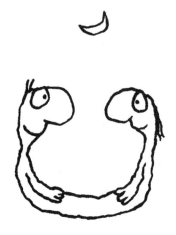

'Love one another and you will be happy.'
It's as simple and difficult as that.
There is no other way.

Amen.

HarperCollins*Publishers*

A Common Prayer first published in 1990
The Prayer Tree first published in 1991
Common Prayer Collection first published in 1993
When I Talk To You, comprising material from *A Common Prayer* and *The Prayer Tree*,
first published in Australia in 2004
by HarperCollins*Publishers* Pty Limited
ABN 36 009 913 517
A member of the HarperCollins*Publishers* (Australia) Pty Limited Group
www.harpercollins.com.au

HarperCollins*Publishers*
25 Ryde Road, Pymble, Sydney, NSW 2073, Australia
31 View Road, Glenfield, Auckland 10, New Zealand
77–85 Fulham Palace Road, London W6 8JB, United Kingdom
2 Bloor Street East, 20th floor, Toronto, Ontario M4W 1A8, Canada
10 East 53rd Street, New York, NY 10022, USA

National Library of Australia Cataloguing-in-Publication data:

Leunig, Michael, 1945– .
    When I talk to you : a cartoonist talks to God.
    ISBN 0 7322 8043 5.
    1. Prayers. I. Leunig, Michael, 1945– . II. Title.

Cover and internal design by Mark Gowing Design
Creative direction by Jenny Grigg, HarperCollins Design Studio
Typeset in Bembo Regular
Printed in Hong Kong by Phoenix Offset on 100gsm Cream Woodfree

6 5 4 3 2 1   04 05 06 07